Odd Animals

Rose Davidson

NATIONAL GEOGRAPHIC

Washington, D.C.

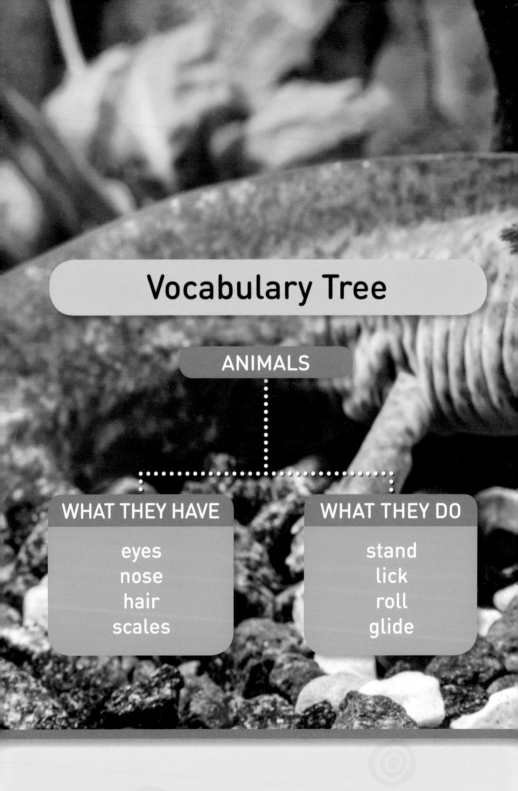

Vocabulary Tree

ANIMALS

WHAT THEY HAVE

eyes
nose
hair
scales

WHAT THEY DO

stand
lick
roll
glide

Mexican axolotl

Animals may look odd.
But odd can be good!

These animals have odd eyes.

tarsiers

barking owl

Big eyes help them see.

This animal has an odd nose.

saiga antelope

It helps the
animal breathe.

Hair can be odd, too!

naked mole rat

hippopotamus

Some animals
have very little hair.

Other animals have lots of hair.

alpaca

cotton-top tamarins

It keeps them
safe and warm.

Sometimes animals have an odd shape.

leafy sea dragon

This animal's
shape helps it hide.

Sometimes animals
do odd things.

Moroccan goats

These animals stand in trees.
They look for food.

Slurp! This animal licks its eyes.

crested gecko

Now they are clean.

This animal rolls into a ball.

pangolin

Scales protect its body.

Swoosh! This animal glides from tree to tree.

flying frog

It finds a place to rest.

Yes, some animals are odd. That's what makes them great!

platypus

ocean sunfish

secretary bird

jerboa

YOUR TURN!

Describe the animals below.
What do they have? What do they do?
Use these words:

stand   lick   glide   hair   nose

For Alex —R.D.

softshell turtle

AUTHOR'S NOTE: The odd animal on the cover of this book is a tarsier. The animal on the first page is an elephant seal. Male elephant seals have big noses!

The author and publisher gratefully acknowledge the expert literacy review of this book by Kimberly Gillow, Principal, Chelsea School District, Michigan.

Designed by Gus Tello

Photo Credits

Cover, lifegallery/Getty Images; 1, Mint Images - Frans Lanting/Getty Images; 2–3, Lapis2380/Shutterstock; 4, Lars Ruecker/Getty Images; 5, Nicole Patience/Shutterstock; 6, Victor Tyakht/Alamy Stock Photo; 7, Victor Tyakht/Shutterstock; 8, Frans Lanting/National Geographic Creative; 9, Roy Toft/National Geographic Creative; 10, Pete Oxford/Nature Picture Library; 11, Marten_House/Shutterstock; 12, GaetanoDGargiulo imagery/Getty Images; 13, Brent Hedges/Nature Picture Library; 14-15, Aerostato/Shutterstock; 16-17, Geoffrey Newland/Shutterstock; 18, Daryl Balfour/Getty Images; 19, Jen Guyton/Nature Picture Library; 20, Quentin Martinez/Biosphoto/Alamy Stock Photo; 21, Ryan M. Bolton/Shutterstock; 22 (UP LE), D. Parer and E. Parer-Cook/Minden Pictures; 22 (UP RT), Sergio Hanquet/Minden Pictures; 22 (LO LE), Michael Potter11/Shutterstock; 22 (LO RT), reptiles4all/Shutterstock; 23 (UP LE), Pete Oxford/Nature Picture Library; 23 (UP RT), Aerostato/ Shutterstock; 23 (CTR LE), Geoffrey Newland/Shutterstock; 23 (CTR RT), Quentin Martinez/Biosphoto/Alamy Stock Photo; 23 (LO), Victor Tyakht/Alamy Stock Photo; 24, Ed Reschke/Getty Images

Library of Congress Cataloging-in-Publication Data

Names: Davidson, Rose M., author. | National Gegraphic Kids (Firm), publisher. | National Geographic Society (U.S.)
Title: Odd animals / by Rose Davidson.
Description: Washington, DC : National Geographic Kids, [2019] | Series: National geographic readers | Audience: Age 2-5. | Audience: Grade pre-school, excluding K.
Identifiers: LCCN 2018035829 (print) | LCCN 2018039021 (ebook) | ISBN 9781426333415 (e-book) | ISBN 9781426333422 (e-book + audio) | ISBN 9781426333392 (paperback) | ISBN 9781426333408 (hardcover)
Subjects: LCSH: Animals--Miscellanea--Juvenile literature.
Classification: LCC QL49 (ebook) | LCC QL49 .D354 2019 (print) | DDC 590--dc23
LC record available at https://lccn.loc.gov/2018035829

National Geographic supports K–12 educators with ELA Common Core Resources. Visit natgeoed.org /commoncore for more information.

Printed in U.S.A.
22/WOR/2